U.S. Regions

The
The People of the
Northeast

Blaine Wiseman

www.av2books.com

AV² provides enriched content that supplements and complements this book. Weigl's AV² books strive to create inspired learning and engage young minds in a total learning experience.

Your AV² Media Enhanced books come alive with...

Audio
Listen to sections of the book read aloud.

Key Words
Study vocabulary, and complete a matching word activity.

Go to **www.av2books.com**, and enter this book's unique code.

BOOK CODE

J 2 2 1 8 9 6

Video
Watch informative video clips.

Quizzes
Test your knowledge.

Embedded Weblinks
Gain additional information for research.

Slide Show
View images and captions, and prepare a presentation.

AV² by Weigl brings you media enhanced books that support active learning.

Try This!
Complete activities and hands-on experiments.

... and much, much more!

Published by AV² by Weigl
350 5th Avenue, 59th Floor
New York, NY 10118

Websites: www.av2books.com   www.weigl.com

Library of Congress Control Number: 2014942118

ISBN 978-1-4896-2848-0 (hardcover)
ISBN 978-1-4896-2459-8 (softcover)
ISBN 978-1-4896-2460-4 (single-user eBook)
ISBN 978-1-4896-2461-1 (multi-user eBook)

Printed in the United States of America in North Mankato, Minnesota
1 2 3 4 5 6 7 8 9 18 17 16 15 14

062014
WEP060614

Project Coordinator: Aaron Carr
Design: Mandy Christiansen

Every reasonable effort has been made to trace ownership and to obtain permission to reprint copyright material. The publishers would be pleased to have any errors or omissions brought to their attention so that they may be corrected in subsequent printings.

Weigl acknowledges Getty Images as its primary image supplier for this title.

Contents

Introducing the Northeast

The Northeast is the smallest of the five regions in the United States. It is, however, one of the most important regions for politics and business. Millions of people live along the Atlantic coast. It is one of the most **densely** populated areas on the planet. New York City is the largest city in the United States. It is located in the Northeast. Washington, D.C. is the nation's capital city. Formed in 1791, it was named for President George Washington.

Washington

Oregon

Montana

Idaho

Wyoming

Nevada

Utah

California

Colorado

Arizona

New Mexico

Pacific Ocean

MEXICO

Legend

- ■ West (11 states)
- ☐ Southwest (5 states)
- ☐ Northeast (11 states)
- ■ Southeast (11 states)
- ▨ Midwest (12 states)

Alaska

0   500 Miles
0   500 Km

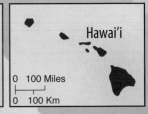

Hawai'i

0   100 Miles
0   100 Km

Where People Live in the West

Compare the populations of the biggest city in each Western state.

City	Population
New York City, **New York**	8,336,697
Philadelphia, **Pennsylvania**	1,547,607
Washington, **D.C.**	646,449
Boston, **Massachusetts**	636,479

CANADA

North Dakota

Minnesota

South Dakota

Wisconsin

Lake Superior

Lake Huron

Lake Ontario

Lake Michigan

Michigan

Lake Erie

New Hampshire

Maine

Vermont

Massachusetts

New York

Rhode Island

Connecticut

Iowa

Indiana

Ohio

Pennsylvania

New Jersey

Nebraska

UNITED STATES

Delaware

Maryland

Kansas

Missouri

Illinois

West Virginia

Virginia

Washington, D.C.

Kentucky

Tennessee

North Carolina

Oklahoma

Arkansas

South Carolina

Georgia

Atlantic Ocean

N

Texas

Alabama

Mississippi

Louisiana

Florida

Gulf of Mexico

0   250 Miles

0   250 Kilometers

City	Population	City	Population
Baltimore, **Maryland**	621,342	Manchester, **New Hampshire**	110,209
Newark, **New Jersey**	277,727	Wilmington, **Delaware**	71,292
Providence, **Rhode Island**	178,432	Portland, **Maine**	66,214
Bridgeport, **Connecticut**	146,425	Burlington, **Vermont**	42,417

*2012 population figures

Settling the Northeast

For thousands of years, the Northeast has been a region of rich cultures and powerful societies. American Indian nations, such as the Iroquois and Algonquian thrived there. Most Northeastern nations built villages centered around agriculture, growing crops such as corn, beans, and squash. These nations were often at war with each other, fighting for land and resources. Their towns were surrounded by large walls for protection.

In the 17th century, people from England started the colonies that would become the first states in the United States of America. European countries such as England, France, and the Netherlands fought for control of the land. The settlements they built grew into the cities and towns we see in the region today.

★ The first Europeans to arrive in America came across the Atlantic Ocean. Explorers such as Henry Hudson, from Great Britain, landed on the far eastern shores of America.

Northeastern Migrations

13,000 BC–AD 1500

After the first people crossed from Asia to North America, they spread throughout the continent. In the Northeast, they settled on the plains, in the forests, and along the coast. By the time Europeans arrived, there were about 100,000 American Indians in **New England**.

1620–1700

In 1620, a few dozen people set up the first New England colony at Plymouth. By 1700, there were around 175,000 people in the colonies of the Northeast. English settlers built the colonies of New England, while the Dutch and Swedish settled around New York.

1846–1851

When Ireland's potato crop was destroyed by a fungus, many people were starving. Many Irish people died, while many others left to find food and work in other countries. In five years, more than 1 million Irish people sailed to the United States. They settled in places such as Boston, Philadelphia, and New York. Today, Irish Americans are the third largest **ethnic** group in the nation.

1892–1954

In the decades after the Civil War, industries in the United States grew to be the strongest in the world. This attracted many new immigrants from all over the world. In just over 60 years, Ellis Island in New York City processed more than 12 million immigrants. Many moved on to other regions, but millions of people settled in Northeastern cities.

1916–1970

Segregation and a poor economy in southern states made life difficult for African Americans. Northeastern cities offered more opportunity and a better life. After the 1910s, and up until about 1970, a time known as the Great Migration saw huge growth in the populations of African Americans in Northeastern cities.

Historic Events

The Northeast has played a major role in shaping the United States. Many of the nation's most important historical events have happened in the region. It has seen vicious wars and violent attacks, and it has seen peace and cooperation between cultures. Through history, Northeasterners have made many important achievements that led to the formation and success of today's nation.

The Mayflower (1620)

In 1620, 102 English immigrants arrived on the shores of Massachusetts in a ship called the *Mayflower*. They spent the first winter living on the ship, where half of them died. The next spring, they began building Plymouth, the first European settlement in New England. Local American Indians helped the colonists survive, teaching them to hunt, fish, and farm in the new land.

Boston Tea Party (1773)

By 1773, many Americans living in the colonies began resisting British laws they felt were unfair, such as the Tea Act. The law placed high taxes on tea in the colonies. A group led by Samuel Adams boarded ships in Boston Harbor and dumped 45 tons (40.8 tonnes) of tea into the water. It was one of the major events that led to the Revolutionary War.

The Shot Heard Round the World (1775)

Tension began rising between Great Britain and the colonies. The colonial army found out that British troops were planning an attack in Concord, Massachusetts. About five hundred colonial revolutionaries met the British troops in Lexington. The first shots of the Revolutionary War were fired there.

Declaration of Independence (1776)

As the Revolutionary War went on, American leaders wanted to make a statement. Thomas Jefferson was chosen to write a document declaring America's independence from Britain. On July 4, in Philadelphia, Congress adopted the Declaration of Independence.

Burning of Washington (1814)

In 1812, U.S. troops attacked and burned the British city of York in Canada. Two years later, the British got their revenge when they overtook the city of Washington. They began setting buildings on fire, including the president's home. The White House was rebuilt between 1815 and 1817.

Battle of Gettysburg (1863)

During the Civil War, 170,000 soldiers fought in a field at Gettysburg, Pennsylvania. More than 50,000 men were killed or wounded in the bloodiest battle of the Civil War. More than one-third of the Lee's army was killed.

The Plymouth colonists signed the Mayflower Compact, the first written form of government in what is now the United States. In 1621, they celebrated the first Thanksgiving, thanking their American Indian neighbors for their help.

A few months after the Battle of Gettysburg, President Lincoln traveled there for a ceremony at the new Gettysburg National Cemetery. It was there that Lincoln made his most famous speech, the Gettysburg Address.

September 11 Attacks (2001)

On September 11, 2001, four airplanes flying out of Boston, Washington, D.C., and Newark airports, were **highjacked**. Two of the planes slammed into New York's World Trade Center towers. Another was crashed into the Pentagon, just outside of Washington. The fourth plane crashed into a field in Pennsylvania. It was the worst terrorist attack in U.S. history, killing 2,996 people.

Historic Northeasterners

Northeasterners have led some of the greatest changes the United States has ever seen. The region has produced some of the country's greatest thinkers, dreamers, and builders. These people have shaped the nation, created some of its greatest art, and changed the world with their ideas.

Benjamin Franklin (1706–1790)

Benjamin Franklin was a writer, inventor, and scientist. He was one of America's **Founding Fathers**. He was born in Boston and moved to Philadelphia. Franklin also worked as a **postmaster** and printer, and conducted important experiments with electricity. Franklin's greatest legacy comes from helping to write the Declaration of Independence and the U.S. Constitution.

Eli Whitney (1765–1825)

Eli Whitney grew up on a farm in Westboro, Massachusetts. In 1793, he invented the cotton gin, a machine that made picking cotton much quicker. Whitney's machine helped the economy grow and inspired other inventors to create farm machinery. He is known as "the father of American technology."

Herman Melville (1819–1891)

Herman Melville was born in New York City. After his family's business failed, he began working as a sailor, and eventually got a job on a whaling ship. He wrote stories about his experiences at sea. It was not until after he died that his final book, *Moby Dick*, became popular. Today, it is considered one of the greatest novels ever written.

Susan B. Anthony (1820–1906)

Susan B. Anthony was born in Adams, Massachusetts. Her family were **Quakers** who taught her the value of hard work and strong morals. Throughout her life, Anthony fought for women's **suffrage** and the **abolition** of slavery. Anthony lived to see abolition, but women were not given the right to vote until 14 years after her death.

Walt Whitman (1819–1892)

Walt Whitman was born in West Hills, New York. He is known as one of the United States' greatest poets. He worked as a teacher, journalist, and newspaper editor. Whitman never stopped working on his poetry book, *Leaves of Grass*. By the time he died, it had grown from 12 poems to more than 300.

Frank Sinatra (1915–1998)

Frank Sinatra was born in Hoboken, New Jersey, and began his singing career in high school. In the 1940s, his career took off. He had hit songs playing on the radio, and he began acting in movies. For more than 50 years, Sinatra performed hit songs such as *My Way*, *Summer Wind*, and *New York, New York*.

Babe Ruth (1895–1948)

Babe Ruth was born in Baltimore, Maryland. He started his career in Boston, but became an American icon in New York. Ruth led the Major Leagues in home runs 12 times. He won four World Series with the New York Yankees, and his record of 714 home runs was not broken until 1974. "The Great Bambino" also spent many years helping charities and set up his own foundation for poor children.

In 1919, Babe Ruth set a record by hitting *29* home runs in a season. The next season, he broke his own record, hitting *54* home runs. A season later, he broke it again, with *59*. Finally, in 1927, Ruth hit *60* homers, a record that stood until 1961.

Cultural Groups

Diverse cultural groups have come together to build the Northeast into the powerful region it is today. From the Iroquois **Confederacy** to today's multicultural cities, it is a region of cultural cooperation. For millions of immigrants, the Northeast was the gateway to the United States. Throughout the Northeast, people of similar backgrounds have settled close together, creating culturally unique neighborhoods.

In the United States today, ceremonies are held to welcome new citizens. These are called naturalization ceremonies.

Cultural Communities

All over the Northeast, different groups celebrate their unique cultures and backgrounds. From African Americans to Chinese immigrants, culture is important to people who live in the Northeast.

Harlem, New York City, New York

During the Great Migration, African Americans began moving into empty apartments in a Manhattan neighborhood called Harlem. In the 1920s, the community was home to artists, writers, and musicians who showed African American culture to the world. Today, 80 percent of Harlemites are African American.

Chinatown, Boston, Massachusetts

Boston is home to a small Chinatown that is more than 130 years old. Poor immigrants could afford homes there in the mid-1800s because it is built on top of an old garbage dump. Today, it is a colorful, cultural neighborhood famous for its shops and restaurants. Of the more than 4,000 people in Boston's Chinatown, about 75 percent are of Asian descent.

Little India, Jersey City, New Jersey

Jersey City's Little India neighborhood is a center of Asian Indian culture in the United States. Indian restaurants and shops, along with festivals, like Diwali and Navratri, are popular with locals and tourists. The area is home to the largest Indian population in the Western **Hemisphere**.

Dutch Country, Lancaster County, Pennsylvania

In the 1720s, a group of people left Europe and settled in Lancaster County, Pennsylvania. Known as Amish, they have traditional beliefs and do not use modern technology such as television, cars, or tractors. Today, there are about 30,000 Amish in Lancaster County, the largest Amish community in the United States.

Major Cities of the Northeast

Some of the best-known cities in the United States are located in the Northeast. Cities such as Boston and Philadelphia are home to millions of people. These cities drive the business and politics of the region, the country, and the world.

Boston is the capital city of Massachusetts and the largest city in New England. It was founded in 1630, and is well known for its history and culture. The statue of George Washington on horseback is the largest sculpture in Boston and is located in the Boston Public Gardens. Boston is home to many universities and, today, it is one of the leading research communities in the world.

Philadelphia, Pennsylvania, is one of the most important cities in U.S. history. It was a central part of the independence movement and home to many of the Founding Fathers. During George Washington's presidency, it was the national capital. The "City of Brotherly Love" gets its name from the Greek words "phileo," and "adelphos."

Washington, D.C. is the nation's capital. To solve the argument over which state should have the capital, it was decided to locate it along the northern shore of the Potomac River, bordering the states of Maryland and Virginia. The federal government moved to Washington in 1800. Today, thousands of politicians and many other people come to the city to help run the country.

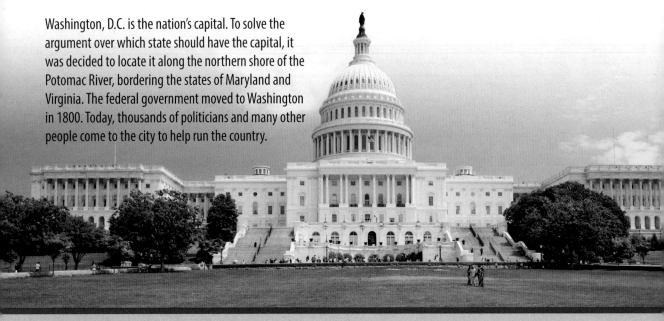

Capital Cities

The capital cities of the Northeast are important cities to the region, the nation, and the world. While some are large, famous cities, others are smaller and less well known. Each of them, though, is home to key leaders and decision-makers.

Baltimore, Maryland, is a city of industry. Its location on the Chesapeake Bay has made it a successful port city for centuries. The city's many factories and mills relied on shipping and railroads to send their goods around the United States and the world. Today, "The Charmed City" is a growing center of technology, medicine, and research.

D.C. *stands for* **District of Columbia.** *There are major differences between a state and a district. D.C. is not represented in Congress the same way states are. The district has no voting power in the U.S. Senate or House of Representatives.*

New York City was the first capital of the United States. There were six other Northeastern cities that served as capital before it moved to Washington. The others were Baltimore, Annapolis, Trenton, Princeton, Lancaster, and York.

State Capitals	Population
Boston, **Massachusetts**	**636,479**
Providence, **Rhode Island**	178,432
Hartford, **Connecticut**	**124,893**
Albany, **New York**	97,904
Trenton, **New Jersey**	**84,477**
Harrisburg, **Pennsylvania**	49,279
Concord, **New Hampshire**	**42,630**
Annapolis, **Maryland**	38,620
Dover, **Delaware**	**37,089**
Augusta, **Maine**	18,946
Montpelier, **Vermont**	7,787

National Capital	Population
Washington, D.C.	646,449

*2012 population figures

Industries of the Northeast

With cities such as New York, Washington D.C., Boston, and Philadelphia, the Northeast plays a major role in the world's economy. Much of the world's money is found in the financial capitals of the region. While natural resources have been important to Northeastern economies, many states are now focused on technology.

Massachusetts

The information technology (IT) industry makes products and programs for computers and other communication tools. It is a growing industry in many states, but especially in Massachusetts.

- **178,000 IT jobs** in the state
- Contributed **$65 billion** to the state in 2008

Vermont

Each year, the United States produces enough maple syrup to fill five Olympic swimming pools. Vermont produces about 40 percent of the sticky pancake topper.

- Vermont had **3.8 million maple syrup taps** in 2012.
- Revenues of **$26 million in 2012**

Delaware

Delaware is a major manufacturer of chemical products. Companies such as DuPont manufacture products in Delaware and sell them all over the world.

- The average chemical engineer in Delaware earns **$124,730**, more than any other state.
- Generated **$1.2 billion** in 2011

Maine

Lobster can be found in coastal waters throughout the Northeast, but Maine lobsters are the most famous. In one year, Maine lobster fishers catch 125 million pounds (56.7 million kilograms) of the shellfish.

- **4,239 lobster harvesters** in Maine in 2013
- **$364 million**—2013 industry value

Pennsylvania

Steel manufacturing has been an important part of Pennsylvania's economy since the 1800s. Its second biggest city, Pittsburgh, is nicknamed "The Steel City."

- **80,000 Pennsylvanians** working in **steel manufacturing**
- Pumped **$9.35 billion** into state economy in 2009

Maryland

Aerospace and defense is an industry that designs and builds airplanes, spaceships, and high-tech weapons. Maryland is one of the leading states in the aerospace and defense industry.

- **91,000 people** employed in **aerospace and defence** in Maryland
- Generated **$21.2 billion** for the state in 2009

New York

New York is the world leader in the financial industry. Most of the finance jobs in the state are in New York City.

- **558,000 jobs in New York's financial sector**
- The average financial worker in New York earns **$182,100 per year**.

New Hampshire

Computer and electronics make up the biggest part of New Hampshire's manufacturing industry.

- **15,800** computer and electronics jobs in state
- Contributed **$2 billion** to state economy in 2009

New Jersey

New Jersey is home to many top pharmaceutical manufacturing companies. These companies make medicine for people all over the world.

- **52,125 pharmaceutical** jobs in New Jersey
- The average pharmaceutical manufacturing worker in New Jersey earns **$134,721 per year**.

Northeastern Tourism

The Northeast is home to a huge number of important historical and cultural sites. While the most famous are located in the region's largest cities, popular attractions can be found in every state.

New York, New York City's Times Square is the most popular tourist attraction in the world. Visitors are amazed by the flashing neon lights and towering skyscrapers of Times Square. Each year, more than 39 million people visit "The Crossroads of the World."

New Hampshire, New Hampshire's White Mountain National Forest covers almost 800,000 acres (323,750 hectares). The White Mountains are part of the Appalachian mountain chain that runs all the way from Canada to Alabama. Visitors are attracted by hiking trails that reach high into the mountains. More than 1.7 million people visit the area every year.

Maine, Acadia National Park was created in 1919, the first national park in the eastern United States. The 47,453-acre (19,203-hectare) park features rocky coastline and towering mountain peaks. A highlight of the park is Cadillac Mountain, where visitors can watch the earliest sunrise in the country. More than 2.4 million people visit the park every year.

Maryland, Assateague Island National Seashore is a series of islands and **islets** off the coast of Maryland. While 850,000 people visit every year, the most famous residents of the island are not people. Wild ponies roam the beaches, and there are more than 300 bird species on the island.

Connecticut, Hammonasset Beach State Park offers visitors a wide variety of activities, with more than 2 miles (3.2 km) of beach to explore. Scuba diving, fishing, and swimming are only some of the activities available at Connecticut's biggest shoreline park. A million people visit the park each year.

Rhode Island, Roger Williams Park Zoo began as a place to display animals in 1872. Today, it focuses on educating the public about the natural world. Located in Providence, it is one of the oldest zoos in the United States. More than 600,000 people visit every year.

Massachusetts, Faneuil Hall was built in 1742 and is one of the most popular tourist attractions in the world. Well-known people such as Samuel Adams, Susan B. Anthony, and Bill Clinton have spoken there. Today, tourists flock to the area for entertainment and shopping. The hall is the centerpiece of Faneuil Hall Marketplace, which attracts 18 million visitors every year.

Each New Year's Eve, almost **1 million people** gather in Times Square to watch the famous ball drop at midnight.

Faneuil Hall is where the phrase, **"No taxation without representation,"** became famous. It came from the colonists wanting more representation in the British government in exchange for paying British taxes.

Famous Northeasterners

Northeasterners love to create and perform. Many well-known actors, authors, and songwriters are from the Northeast United States. These famous people have continued the Northeastern traditions of telling great stories and making their mark on the United States and the world.

Stephen King was born in Portland, Maine, in 1947. Known for his scary subjects, King is one of the most successful authors in the world. More than 350 million copies of his books have sold, and many have been turned into popular TV shows and movies.

Judy Blume is one of America's favorite writers for teenagers and children. She was born in Elizabeth, New Jersey, in 1938, and spent her childhood making up stories. Her books deal with real issues faced by kids. Books, such as *Blubber*, *Tiger Eyes*, and *Are You There, God? It's Me, Margaret,* have been read by millions of people around the world. Blume's books have sold more than 38 million copies.

Stan Lee is famous but his characters are much more well known than he is. Lee was born in New York City in 1922. During World War II, he worked as a writer and illustrator. Working at Marvel Comics, he created some of the world's most famous superheroes.

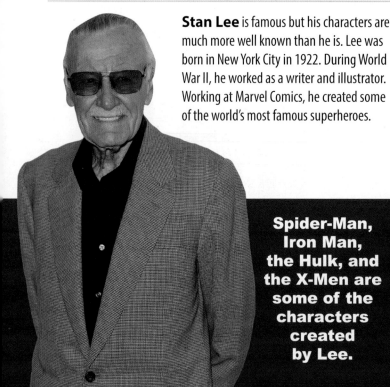

Spider-Man, Iron Man, the Hulk, and the X-Men are some of the characters created by Lee.

Jack Nicholson was born in 1937 and grew up in Manasquan, New Jersey. His acting career began in 1954, and Nicholson has become one of the most famous and popular actors in the United States. He has appeared in classic movies such as *Easy Rider*, *Chinatown*, *The Shining*, and *One Flew Over the Cuckoo's Nest*. Nicholson has won three Academy Awards for Best Actor.

Bruce Springsteen was born in 1949 in Long Branch, New Jersey. He grew up in nearby Freehold Borough. He began playing guitar when he was 16, and has become famous worldwide. Hits such as *Born to Run*, *Born in the U.S.A.*, and *Streets of Philadelphia*, tell stories of life and struggle in the United States. Throughout his career, Springsteen has sold more than 123 million albums.

Born in 1970 in Huntington, New York, **Mariah Carey** began taking singing lessons when she was only 4 years old. In the 1990s, she became one of the world's most popular singers, with hits such as *Hero* and *Fantasy*. Carey is the third best-selling female musician in history, with more than 160 million album sales around the world.

Shawn Carter was born in Brooklyn, New York, and grew up surrounded by drugs and crime. He began rapping in high school, trying to stay out of trouble, and took the stage name, Jay Z. In 1996, he started his own record label and began releasing albums. Jay Z also owns his own clothing line, a film company, and the Brooklyn Nets basketball team. He has sold more than 55 million albums.

Northeastern Politics

The Northeast is a region built on politics. It is where the United States and its politics were born. In Washington, the nation's leaders make decisions that affect every citizen of the United States. Northeasterners have been some of the greatest leaders in the country's history.

John Adams was born in Massachusetts in 1735. At the time, Massachusetts was a colony. Adams was a leader of the Independence movement, and served as vice president for George Washington. Adams became president in 1797, and in 1800, became the first leader of the nation to live in the White House.

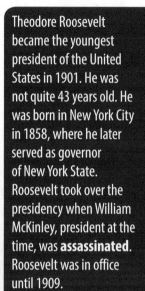

Theodore Roosevelt became the youngest president of the United States in 1901. He was not quite 43 years old. He was born in New York City in 1858, where he later served as governor of New York State. Roosevelt took over the presidency when William McKinley, president at the time, was **assassinated**. Roosevelt was in office until 1909.

Franklin D. Roosevelt, a cousin of Theodore Roosevelt, was born in Hyde Park, New York, in 1882. In 1921, the rising politician became ill and had to spend most of his life afterward in a wheelchair. Not letting his handicap slow him down, Roosevelt became president in 1933 during the Great Depression. His "New Deal" helped pull the nation out of poverty, and he served until 1945.

John F. Kennedy was born in Brookline, Massachusetts, in 1917. He graduated from Harvard in 1940. During World War II, he served in the navy and became a war hero for his bravery. After the war, he served as a congressman and senator before becoming president in 1961. A strong leader, Kennedy was assassinated after less than three years as president.

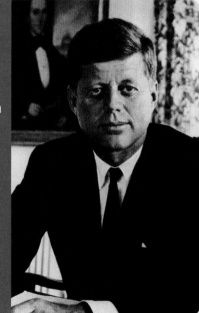

State Politics

While both of the political parties in the United States have supporters in the Northeast, most of the region votes for the Democratic Party. In the 2012 election, all of the states in the region voted in favor of the Democrats.

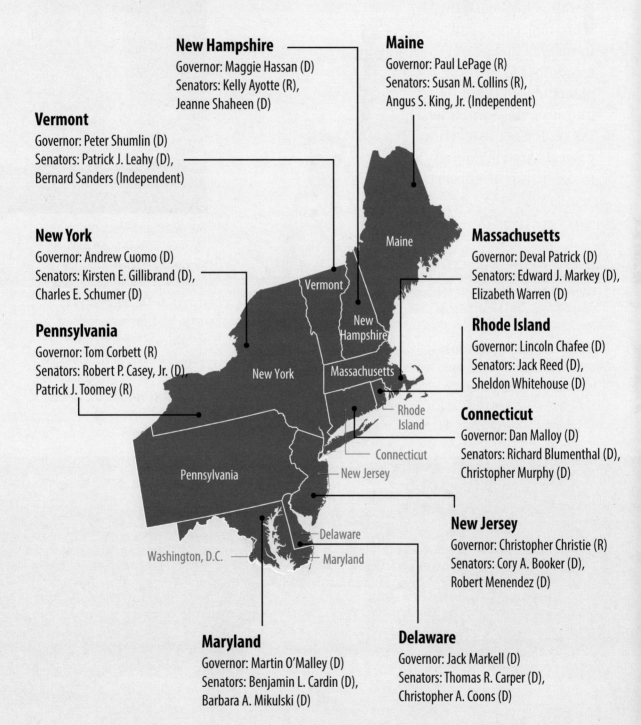

New Hampshire
Governor: Maggie Hassan (D)
Senators: Kelly Ayotte (R),
Jeanne Shaheen (D)

Maine
Governor: Paul LePage (R)
Senators: Susan M. Collins (R),
Angus S. King, Jr. (Independent)

Vermont
Governor: Peter Shumlin (D)
Senators: Patrick J. Leahy (D),
Bernard Sanders (Independent)

New York
Governor: Andrew Cuomo (D)
Senators: Kirsten E. Gillibrand (D),
Charles E. Schumer (D)

Massachusetts
Governor: Deval Patrick (D)
Senators: Edward J. Markey (D),
Elizabeth Warren (D)

Pennsylvania
Governor: Tom Corbett (R)
Senators: Robert P. Casey, Jr. (D),
Patrick J. Toomey (R)

Rhode Island
Governor: Lincoln Chafee (D)
Senators: Jack Reed (D),
Sheldon Whitehouse (D)

Connecticut
Governor: Dan Malloy (D)
Senators: Richard Blumenthal (D),
Christopher Murphy (D)

New Jersey
Governor: Christopher Christie (R)
Senators: Cory A. Booker (D),
Robert Menendez (D)

Maryland
Governor: Martin O'Malley (D)
Senators: Benjamin L. Cardin (D),
Barbara A. Mikulski (D)

Delaware
Governor: Jack Markell (D)
Senators: Thomas R. Carper (D),
Christopher A. Coons (D)

Maine
Vermont
New Hampshire
New York
Massachusetts
Rhode Island
Connecticut
New Jersey
Pennsylvania
Delaware
Maryland
Washington, D.C.

Monuments and Buildings

In the Northeast, there are many moments in history that are remembered by the placement of large monuments. Sometimes, the region's construction projects are big enough to make history themselves.

The Washington Monument is a 555-foot (169-m) tower honoring George Washington. It is in the city named for him. Construction started in 1848, but money ran out in 1854. The monument was completed between 1876 and 1884. At the time, it was the tallest structure of its kind. Visitors can ride an elevator to the top and look out over the nation's capital.

The Statue of Liberty was a gift to the United States from the people of France. While the base was being built on Liberty Island, the statue was built in France. Lady Liberty was taken apart before she sailed across the ocean and was rebuilt in New York. The 305.5-foot (93.1-meter), 225-ton (204-tonne) statue was officially completed in 1886.

On July 8, 1776, the bell at the top of Independence Hall in Philadelphia rang out, celebrating the country's independence. Built 25 years earlier, the copper and tin bell cracked during a test and was repaired twice. It was used to announce and celebrate important events. By 1846, the bell, now known as the Liberty Bell, was cracked again. Today, the Liberty Bell is one of the greatest symbols of the country's independence.

When New York Governor Dewitt Clinton proposed the idea for the Erie Canal in 1808, people thought it was impossible. When it was completed in 1925, the canal was considered the greatest engineering achievement in the United States. The canal runs for 363 miles (587 km)—from the Hudson River to Lake Erie, connecting the Atlantic Ocean with the Great Lakes.

Construction began on the White House in 1792 as part of George Washington's plan for a new United States' capital city. Since 1800, it has served as the official home of every president. It was not given the name "White House" until 101 years after it was built, when Theodore Roosevelt moved in and officially named it. Today, the White House also serves as a museum of U.S. history, with 6,000 visitors every day.

One World Trade Center is the tallest building in the United States, and the fourth tallest in the world. The 104-story, 1,776-foot (541.3-m) tower stands where the Twin Towers stood until the September 11, 2001, terrorist attacks. Using state-of-the-art technology, it is one of the safest buildings ever constructed.

Flags and Seals

Many of the flags and seals of the Northeastern states are based on those of the colonies that came before them. They feature the symbols and designs that show the values of the states and their people. Flags and seals can be found at state government buildings and on other important properties.

Delaware

Flag The state seal is inside a yellow diamond on a background of blue. The diamond represents Thomas Jefferson calling Delaware a "jewel" of the states.

Seal The seal represents the ships that carried settlers to the colonies. The ox, wheat, corn, and a farmer holding a hoe show the agriculture of the state, and the militiaman holding a musket is a tribute to Delaware's revolutionary soldiers.

New Jersey

Flag The New Jersey flag features the images from the state seal on a yellow-brown background.

Seal The horse is the official state animal. Its head is featured on the seal. It symbolizes speed and strength. The helmet stands for **sovereignty**, and the Lady Liberty for freedom.

Maryland

Flag The flag shows the **coat-of-arms** of George Calvert, Lord Baltimore, founder of Maryland. The black and gold colors are symbols of the Calvert family.

Seal Only the back of the seal is used officially. The front shows George Calvert dressed as a knight on horseback. The back of the seal features the words "Scuto bonae voluntatis tuae coronasti nos" which mean, "You have crowned us with the shield of your goodwill." The velvet cloak and crowns show royalty, and a farmer shows Maryland's agriculture.

Rhode Island

Flag Images from the state seal are on a white background. The 13 stars represent the original 13 Colonies.

Seal The anchor stands for hope for "the Ocean State," and "Hope" is the official state **motto**. The Rhode Island colony was founded in 1636.

Massachusetts

Flag The flag features the images from the state seal on a white background.

Seal The seal features the phrases, "Sigillum Reipublicae Massachusettensis," which means "Seal of the State of Massachusetts," and the state's motto, "Ense Petit Placidam Sub Libertate Quietem," which means "By the sword we seek peace, but peace only under liberty".

Connecticut

Flag The flag shows a shield with images from the state seal on a blue background.

Seal The three grapevines on the seal represent happiness, liberty, and peace, as well as the three colonies that came together to form Connecticut.

Pennsylvania

Flag Pennsylvania's coat of arms is on a blue background. The horses show a readiness to serve the country. "Virtue, Liberty, and Independence" is Pennsylvania's motto.

Seal On the front of the seal is an eagle, which stands for American protection. The corn represents agricultural riches, and the olive branch means peace. The back shows Lady Liberty standing over a lion, and the words, "Both Can't Survive," which means liberty over **tyranny**.

New York

Flag The flag shows images from the state seal on a blue background.

Seal The eagle on the seal stands for American protection and the globe shows America and Europe, bringing the Old and New Worlds together.

Vermont

Flag The flag shows images from the state seal on a blue background.

Seal The seal has wavy lines, which show the sky and water of the state. The fallen **fleur-de-lis** represents the passing of Vermont from French to British control in 1763.

New Hampshire

Flag The state seal is represented on a blue background.

Seal The seal shows a laurel wreath, which represents victory. The rising sun represents hope. There is also the ship "Raleigh". This was the first ship in the U.S. Navy, and the first to carry the American flag into battle.

Maine

Flag The state seal is featured on a blue background.

Seal The Polar Star on the seal shows Maine as the guiding star for its people. "Dirigo" is Maine's motto, standing for "I Guide," in Latin. The moose is Maine's official animal.

Challenges Facing the Northeast

Warming It Up

As the world gets warmer, sea levels rise and weather patterns change. This is a major concern in the Northeast. With more than 50 million people in the region, natural disasters such as floods, droughts, and hurricanes could harm millions. Hotter weather can make air pollution in big cities worse. **Smog** is already a problem. More smog can make it difficult for people to breathe and cause illnesses such as lung cancer.

Another climate change problem in the Northeast is that the region gets more rain and less snow than before. The combination of water and heat helps mosquitoes breed. These insects can spread diseases between people. Changing weather is also bad for crops. As the region warms up, crops that grow there now may not grow in the future. Two important Northeastern crops at risk are cranberries and maple syrup.

Breaking It Up

One of the largest natural gas fields in the world is between 5,000 and 8,000 feet (1,524 and 2,438 meters) below the ground in Pennsylvania. This vast natural resource is an important part of the economy. While it could support more than 200,000 jobs in the state, some people want to stop the industry.

⭐ A containment pond can be used to hold and treat toxic water that is carried to the surface by natural gas.

A high-tech process called hydraulic fracturing is used to get natural gas out of the ground. After drilling a hole thousands of feet (meters) below the surface, fluid is then pumped into it. The high pressure of this fluid cracks the **shale rock**, releasing gas. Hydraulic fracturing is good for the oil and gas industry, but there are problems with it. Fracturing fluid contains toxic chemicals that can be harmful if they get into drinking water. Another problem is that fracturing can cause earthquakes. While people need natural gas for fuel, it is also important to protect the environment. Finding the safest way of getting fuel out of the ground will benefit everyone.

⭐ Global warming has made the environment warmer and more moist than in the past. This kind of climate change can cause weather events, such as storms, that disrupt life and damage property in Northeastern cities.

Average yearly temperatures have risen by **2°F** to **4°F** (1.12°C to 2.24°C) in the Northeast since the 1970s.

More than 350,000 oil and gas wells have been drilled in Pennsylvania since 1859.

Quiz

1 How many American Indians were in New England when Europeans first arrived?

2 Where was the first national capital city of the United States?

3 Who gave the Statue of Liberty to America?

4 Who led the Boston Tea Party?

5 Which national seashore is home to wild ponies?

6 Who started America's first hospital?

7 Where is largest Amish community in the United States?

8 Who created the X-Men?

9 Which two Northeastern presidents were cousins?

10 Who founded Maryland?

ANSWERS: 1. 100,000 **2.** New York City **3.** The people of France **4.** Samuel Adams **5.** Assateague Island National Seashore **6.** Benjamin Franklin **7.** Lancaster County, Pennsylvania **8.** Stan Lee **9.** Theodore and Franklin D. Roosevelt **10.** George Calvert, Lord Baltimore

Key Words

abolition: to make something illegal

assassinated: murdered for political reasons

coat-of-arms: a shield showing the symbols of a people or a place

Confederacy: an alliance between groups

densely: packed close together

ethnic: cultural

fleur-de-lis: a flower symbol of France

Founding Fathers: political leaders of the United States who signed the Declaration of Independence

hemisphere: side of the world

highjacked: taken control of

islets: small islands

motto: a slogan or catch phrase that shows the values and beliefs of a person, place, or organization

New England: an area made up of Maine, New Hampshire, Vermont, Massachusetts, Connecticut, and Rhode Island

postmaster: the person in charge of the post office

Quakers: a religious group who believe in peace

segregation: to keep two things apart, such as two groups of people

shale rock: a kind of rock that is made up of layers of clay pressed together with other small particles of mineral matter

smog: smoky fog, air pollution caused by factories and cars

sovereignty: the power of a nation to lead itself

suffrage: the right to vote

tyranny: a cruel government

Index

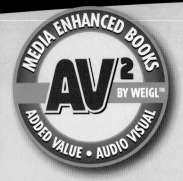

Log on to www.av2books.com

AV² by Weigl brings you media enhanced books that support active learning. Go to www.av2books.com, and enter the special code found on page 2 of this book. You will gain access to enriched and enhanced content that supplements and complements this book. Content includes video, audio, weblinks, quizzes, a slide show, and activities.

AV² Online Navigation

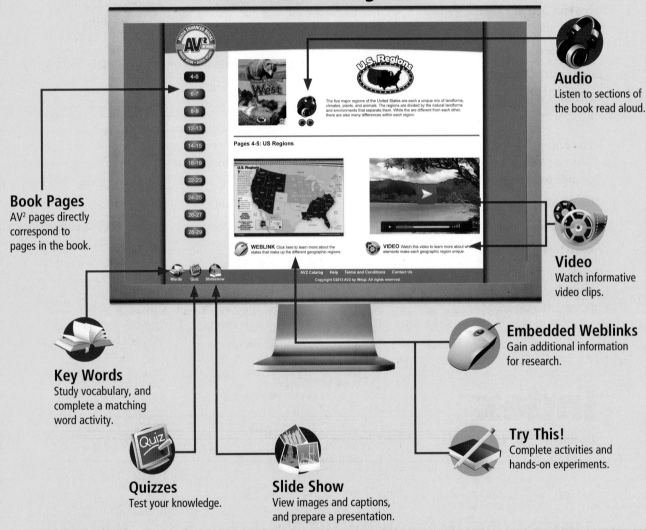

Audio
Listen to sections of the book read aloud.

Book Pages
AV² pages directly correspond to pages in the book.

Video
Watch informative video clips.

Key Words
Study vocabulary, and complete a matching word activity.

Embedded Weblinks
Gain additional information for research.

Quizzes
Test your knowledge.

Slide Show
View images and captions, and prepare a presentation.

Try This!
Complete activities and hands-on experiments.

AV² was built to bridge the gap between print and digital. We encourage you to tell us what you like and what you want to see in the future.

Sign up to be an AV² Ambassador at www.av2books.com/ambassador.